Driving 'n Dreaming

Rotha J. Dawkins

Driving 'n Dreaming

This book is a work of original poetry by
Rotha J. Dawkins.

Copyright @ 2001 by Rotha J. Dawkins
Library of Congress Catalog Number

ISBN: 1-891461-05-2
First Printing: April 2001

Your Treasure Publications
Printed in the United States of America

Driving 'n Dreaming

Original Selected Poems

By
Rotha J. Dawkins

Published by Your Treasure Publications
Lexington, NC
2001

Acknowledgments

A.L. (Red) Johnson for the use of his
beautiful show truck; President and Owner of
Shelba D. Johnson Trucking, Inc.,
Thomasville, NC

Regis Koloshinsky, Director of Maintenance,
Shelba D. Johnson Trucking, Inc.,

Rebekah Tredway,
Executive Photographer and Designer (cover)

Chad Gallimore,
Model and Photo assistant

Carol Agee,
Shelba D. Johnson Trucking, Inc.

Mike Marsh,
Shelba D. Johnson Trucking, Inc.

Agnes Hussey Stevens,
Secretary

Dedication

A.L. (Red) Johnson
Owner-President
Shelba D. Johnson Trucking, Inc.

To my friend, Red Johnson, who has been a real support to me.

Red has always exhibited that special extended hand to all people who know him. He is truly the truckers' trucker. Red started in the business as a young man. His perception of the industry has combined furniture and trucking to a multi-million dollar business. With all that importance, he is never too busy to care and know his friends. Ultimately, Red is loved by all who surround him.

My thanks for your confidence. These pages may reflect some of your times on the road.

This is the beautiful truck on the cover.
Owner: A.L. (Red) Johnson, Thomasville, NC

Contents

Contents *(continued)*

PART I

From

the

Road

My First Love

I look her over from head to tail.
   She's so beautiful, a ten on the scale.
The marvelous color that I chose
   Sultry and pleasant, the finest nose!

The money is out there, I have no doubt.
   I should know our first time out!
Standing back, admiring my dove;
   This sweet truck is my first true love!

Be Still My Love

Be still my love,
    Don't tell me you're going.
Please just let me
    Hang on to you 'til morning!
Go to sleep my love,
    Let me watch over you.
Let the peace swell through your being
    As I comfort you.

Be still my love,
    Hear the spirit linger around.
Let me touch you gently
    With such tenderness profound.
Close your eyes my love,
    and feel the exciting rush.
Just feel good in my comfort
    As if with an angel's blush.

Be still my love,
    Throw all your worries aside.
Let me carry you gently;
    Let our two hearts collide.
Give me a chance
    To follow my every dream.
Be still my love,
    You are my everything!

Ode to Dreams

I then set sail
    With empty palms . . .
A forging force
    With no qualms!
Master of my being
    bids farewell,
Now searching
    for a place to dwell.
Having not the comforts
    for all of life's plan;
Stripped near naked,
    a sad old man.
Still in the far horizon
    I think I see,
A hand of thunder
    coming to rescue me!
Be still, be kind, be happy,
    be sad or dull;
Think! Remember . . .
    rewards are just null.
The destiny of the grave
    is yet not so clear
Keep driving and dreaming
    Find comfort, not fear.

Trucker's Prayer

When all else falls through
    And its just me and you;
I come to my knees, Lord,
    Begging for miracles you do.
I seem now to have come
    to the end of my ropes,
Nothing else much matters,
    I can't seem to find hope.
This world I travel over
    Gets bigger each day.
I work hard and struggle
    While trying to find my way.
It all seems so glib,
    So near pointless indeed.
Let me give them this one load,
    Lord, then, just set me free.

When all else falls through
    And its just me and you;
I come to my knees, Lord,
    Begging for miracles you do.
I loose my self as I travel
    In bleakness and so alone.
I look for a kind of fulfillment
    That might ring out a song.
The little things I ask for
    Seem only to pass me by.
I need a down deep feeling...

To help me survive.
Lord, are you there watching;
    Are you there for my needs?
Are you there to show me
    In this disillusionment and grief?

When all else falls through
    And its just me and you;
I come to my knees, Lord,
    Begging for miracles you do.
I've seen the mountains,
    Winding streams and trails,
The leaves so perfect green
    Turn autumn, as it all unveils.
The barren scope of the desert,
    Freezing and snow up North.
Hollow valleys and canyons
    Are part of the course.
Well, excuse me Lord,
    That's the miracle I've missed.
You are here for me!
    You've touched it with your kiss!

Thank you. Amen.

Oh, How I Need You So

I cherish a flamboyant moment...
When I see you walk in a room
To know that I'm the one you love,
I sing a happy tune,
That brightens up my pathway...
From then until you go,
And when you are near me
Oh, Darling, now I need you so.

Each placid chore that makes me move
Along a routine of time,
Cannot compare to being aware
Of wanting the wedding bell chime.
For when you are there
Standing by strong as it goes...
Oh, sweet, wonderful, beautiful darling...
Oh, love, I need you so.

On Down the Road

We've been out here together
  Over the hills, through the veil of light --
Moving the freight all over,
  In the darkness and inside the night.
Although our highways take us everywhere
  I still pass your winning smile
It's as if you're always there knowing
  While we keep running thousands of miles.

Sometimes we pause to greet each other,
  Taking care to serve the 'beast';
I fuel mine -- you fuel yours –
  Checking it all to say the least.
Inside, there's some comfort in laughter,
  We take turns using the phones,
The meal is pitched, rather off handedly --
  As we brag about what we have at home.

We drop the tip down to the table
  Leave, as no one can really care.
A struggle for feeling more able now
  To run more miles as we should dare.
The midnight comes on with new music
  To brighten my hours with the theme --
But its only meant to keep me rolling
  Dock after dock, fulfilling 'their' dreams.

It gets so lonely, I feel nothing,
  Familiar faces fade through the days,
A touch from someone who loves me --
  Could end all the mist of the craze.
Finally, I see ten eighteen's on the horizon -
  We throw our hands to each as we pass.
Finally, I'm grateful as I roll down my avenue,
  Thank God! I'm really home at last!

7

Truck Driving Man

When the sun rises and night passes on,
I grab my clothes, coffee and phone.
It's time to run . . .To beat the trail.
Several good hours to roll like hell.
It feels great hearing the big engine roar --
We run together out the double door.
We catch the line moving toward the big road
Going north, south, east and west with each load.
No time to eat, just grab a fast snack,
Promising myself something great coming back.

The road looms rapidly ahead with every mile,
I look all around me remembering your smile.
Day after day this pace overwhelms me --
Sometimes, I wonder if it really should be;
Yet each time I deliver, it's someone's big score
The stone in my heart melts like before.
For that instant when they command,
I know it's worth being a truck driving man!

Gladly, then I go on about my rig;
Moving the load as if part of a gig.
We say sweet nothings as we complete the act --
Then, again, I'm dismissed to join the pack.
I do my log and throw it on the dash,
Happy I'm done, I've made my cash!
Driving back, I find the right road --
Now, again, I'm ready for my very next load.
Where I go and for how long it will be --
A truck driving man! That's me!

I Like to Remember

I like to remember the beautiful times
and caress my soul with happy thoughts.
I like to remember the good times,
and nourish the feeling they brought.
I like to remember your deep, sensuous eyes
that enchant me with their lingering love.
I like to remember how you hold me closely
as I send a small prayer above!
I like to remember our promise...
that maybe some tomorrow may bring.
I like to remember each precious feeling
that used to make my heart sing.

I like to remember the sweet touch of love
that you brought to my heart.
I like to remember how beautiful it was
right from the very start.
I like to remember the first time
I met you and became aware.
I like to remember your gentle nature
and even the color of your hair.
I like to remember our promise...
that maybe sometime tomorrow may bring.
I like to remember each precious feeling
that used to make my heart sing.

I Like to Remember *(continued)*

I like to remember days gone by,
of silent moments walking by your side.
I like to remember to tell you
just how you made my heart with yours fly!
I like to remember the way you walk
and your sweet sexy smile.
I like to remember how tall you are
and feel quite like a child.
I like to remember our promise...
that maybe sometime tomorrow may bring.
I like to remember each precious feeling
that used to make my heart sing.

I like to remember your hands
and dream of them clinging to me.
I like to remember deep moments
that only meant the love that we see.
I like to remember that you are good,
that you are more than everything.
I like to remember your strength
and that this was no simple fling.
Yes, how I like to remember our promise,
and I pray that tomorrow will bring,
A time to recapture each precious feeling
and again together our hearts will sing.

More Than Friends

Some taunt you with dying love;
Some scream it to that above...
Special friends are a slender few;
Always there, just for you!
It's all about such moments special
Deeds of care, wonderful and precious!
To run that road at hell's pace;
Then come in and find your place.
Oft times they claim to be tough and bad...
Underneath 'special' reigns so glad!
To share late meals in the middle of the night;
Bring wild morsels that feel so right...
Reaching out with that helping hand,
Always there for when you can...
Sharing time that searches for truth;
Like a slumber party from your youth!
Who else could bother, who else could care?
Who else listens to your dreams that's quare?
Knock on the door and slip coffee through...
Then, add a doughnut to the special brew!
Moments like this can pull you from hell...
This gesture says, "All is well!"
People are just empty shells...
Only filled with special cells...
If someone touches a certain bell...
Pouring out stimulation well!

No need we have, greater than love...
Regardless the form, if from above!
The die be cast that is a heart...
It's all there, right from the start!
Our life hovers in space, 'til we are born...
Ultimately we reach to the storm!
It's not simple at it's own mood...
What sparks glory to break through!
You look for wisdom, acceptance, praise...
Free from error in a candid way!
Someone to be there at all time...
Someone's support, even your crime!
When time passes on to endless places...
When you return there are those faces!
Marked with time that they give...
Perfecting bitterness that you live!
What is so overwhelming to the very end...
We share something that's more than friends!

Finding Love

Then, I felt life slipping away again --
Just please one more day again!
Then I stopped it all and pray again
Now began all over again!

Each moment may be an eternity
That fills our worthwhile need.
To breath erotic pleasure incredibly
And link with its pleasurable seed.
To speak softly sweet words
With keen overtures and meaning
To give love for the taking
And shallow of natural greed.

A good song may be an answer
To heat the heartbeat's insight
To know erotic pleasure is incredible
And feel it's peaceful height!
To love softly with sweet words
With overtures of being right
Then bow down to the surface
And cry out in the night!

Once more, to find love again --
With life to begin again
A very in-depth friend again!
To love, to live, to touch again!

A Prayer for You

When I see the tail lights
    Disappear from sight,
I know you're out there running
    Far into the night.
Nestling deep in my pillows
    From a shadow within;
I whisper God's speed and protection
    Until you're home again.

In Search of Red High Heels
(From <u>Red High Heels II</u>)

That night I tossed
Oh, God how I turned
The name of my beauty
I never had learned.

I couldn't eat and
I could hardly sleep.
Lordy, I beg hard for mercy
All I could do was weep!

I pictured that long red hair
falling to her shoulders
The swing in her move
just purely knocked me over.

A tight, sexy skirt
beneath a business suit so real.
And the strangest touch of all
was seeing those Red High Heels.

I'll search here and the whole world over
I have to search for this four leaf clover.
She wasn't a mirage, she truly was there
I know she'll be someplace, and find her with
care.

One special day
I was staring while fueling the deal,
In the truck right next to me
I saw those Red High Heels.

Her beautiful legs ascended
She came walking up to me
My heart stopped, then pounded --
Red High Heels became my reality!

Chorus
I saw her in the distance
my heart flipped a thrill
I looked that woman over
and saw her Red High Heels!

Shift the Blame

Can you not just face it square?
 Can you not just admit the problem bare?
Simple 'sorry' for silly deeds,
 Unnecessary if you just be free!
Why mask little stupid things,
 Just do what the moment brings!
For what matters, it's all the same...
 Why skirt a fact and shift the blame?

It ought to be right easy,
 To let life flow so breezy!
Let the truth stand on it's own,
 Instead of lying not to be wrong.
A fool just makes claims that others shun;
 He hangs his head and wishes to run.
For what matters, it's all the same...
 Why skirt the fact and shift the blame?

Sometimes it seems the smart thing to be...
 Perfectly right for all others to see!
Yet, the tone of the hours
 Comes with broken power...
And an off-beat circumstance breaks...
 To quibble sour notes and strange leaks!
For what matters, it's all the same...
 Why skirt the truth and shift the blame?

Shift the Blame *(continued)*

People come and people go...
    Some don't have their ducks in a row!
So when the trouble seems not to make sense
    They act so cocky with such pretense.
Along that line for everyone to see...
    You really don't pull it off so easily!
For what matters, it's all the same...
    Why skirt the truth and shift the blame?

Never Down that Road Again

I have given it all to you...
        I reached to the depth of your soul...
I thought we would last forever...
        I gave it all and lost control.
It's like a man loves you best
        If you give him the reigns...
Don't just put it on the line,
        Your life can turn into a bitter thing.
That 'promise' that he will only love you,
        Puts everything in jeopardy...
Then next you'll look and see...
        It's over, gone; you go separately!

I looked to your deep ocean eyes...
        I heard all your troubles besides!
I only thought this should be forever
        Somehow we could band together...
When I opened my weeping eyes
        I found you were again gone!
I felt at that very moment,
        "How could I ever carry on?"
I tried to reason with myself,
        Somehow time would take it away...
But in all I see and everything I do,
        I still hope and foolishly pray!

Never Down that Road Again *(continued)*

It was like we were wrapped away,
　Away from the troubles of broken past!
It was as if your love surrounded me...
　With a passion that would forever last!
I still remember all the words surrendered
　Telling me, "I want you again, and again!"
You must've laughed knowing I was a fool
　Following you down that road again!
But now it's over, you left me behind...
　　You've moved on into your other world!
But for all the love that we shared then...
I back off remembering I was never your girl!

Chorus:
　Never down that road again!
　Never pass the line beyond just friends!
　It doesn't pay to give your heart,
　Stay cold and collected from the start!
　Never down that road again...
　Never down that hurting road again!

Now and Then

There once was a truck that worked so hard,
Now it lays wasting in my side yard.
First went the battery; a friend took a tire…
Next sold the trailer, no longer for hire!
I felt a tear gently slip from my eye;
I knew it was over, truckin' put aside.
Still, memories go forever of days back when,
We met for coffee, braggin' of now and then!

PART II

About

the

Heart

Do We Dare to Love?

A moment...
   Silence...
      An explosion...
        A smile...
          Touch...
            Almost collision!

A man...
   And woman...
      Eye to eye...
        They reach...
          They feel...
            Certain vibes!

Do we dare to love?
Do we take that chance?
Should we not avoid such romance?
Is it fair to want?
Is it right to part?
Should we step that thin line?
Would it be wrong, maybe one time?
Can it be so grand as it would seem?
In the end, what would it mean?
Shall we take each other like never before?
Do we really chance to know the score?
Can you remove your heart like a glove?
Is it possible, do we dare to love?

Can You be the One?

Can you be the one,
Who takes my hand in the shadow,
Then leads me
Into the eternal bliss?
The one, who caresses my being
That lingers with me
And, who in shallow longing...
Soothes me with just a kiss?

Can you be the one,
Who can somehow convince me,
Life itself is really there,
And uplifting the eternal bliss?
The one who stands beside me
So strong and gallant,
Pleading to me, hang on --
Again, to soothe me with a kiss?

Can you be the one,
That I want to remember
Not from the days of past...
But the dream of tomorrow's eternal bliss?
The one, who smiles life
In these breath-taking moments
Who melted the hatred with passion
And serves me a simple kiss?

Can You be the One? *(continued)*

Can you be the one,
Who reaches out carefully,
Without some selfish plan?
Yet, expelling eternal bliss!
Someone propping my soul
With staves strong enough to hang to
And push me to heaven's end...
That man that blows that special kiss?

Can you be the one,
Who walks the fires of fate
With me through even hell's unrest,
Keeping pace, upholding eternal bliss?
That one, to lean on,
To mend all disillusion,
And pursue rich dreams gently...
As you cover me with a kiss?

Can you be the one,
Who makes my heart
Search deep beneath the soul,
To find the realness of true bliss?
The one, I cling desperately to,
The one I give my love,
The one my secrets are safe with
And my world is truly your kiss?

Moments We Shared

Oh for those moments we shared...
Your gentle hand...
Your own special smile...
Your sadness before it began!
I remember all the moments we shared...
You were someone special...I was aware.
It was everything that I needed...
Yet, maybe we were too greedy...
When we stole those moments we shared...
Now it's a memory! But for then, we cared.

Maybe I will always love you,
It was always tedious to tell you so.
Could it have really mattered?
Wish we had never let go!
But all this crazy distance
And the time you have to be gone...
Keeps me hoping someday...
You will find your way back home.
Oh, Baby, those moments we shared,
Will always be an intricate part of me.
Oh, Love, it is all stored away
Maybe someday we will be free.

I remember each detail we shared,
It was as if we were spared,
A masterful feeling of being complete...
In the things you did; then, repeat!
I was looking for nothing
Then you came along...
Sitting there with passion on your mind...
Whistling your song!
I saw your face, I heard your voice...
When you winked, I had no choice!
Oh, Baby...I will always remember the
moments...
The moments we shared...

Chorus:
In my lifetime...There will be none better...
Than, the moments we shared!
Moments so sweet...Moments so tender...
Those moments made my heart surrender...
My love...Lost love...Forever I'll remember
The moments we shared!

Together Alone

It's about two lonely people,
   Playing the old married game...
In two separate worlds
   About to go insane.
The grass needs mowing,
   Still all the bills get paid.
The years keep moving on
   The world says they have it made.
Together -- alone, over morning coffee
   They have nothing to say.
So, he goes to the office,
   And she goes to her day.

Together -- alone; what a way for living
   Together -- alone; just nobody giving.
The kids are grown; now it's together alone
   And this emptiness just makes for
   no home-sweet-home.

These two lonely people
   Keeping up the cold front;
Him chasing his dreams
   And her pride is ruined.
Together they follow
   The routine of time --
Wishing it were all different
   With a heavy loaded mind.
He goes to the office
   She moves about her day --
Together -- alone over morning coffee
   They have nothing to say.

My Dream is Gone

What I wanted could never be,
  You keep your love so far from me.
The mirror of love from your eyes that shine,
  Keeps me feeling that you should be mine!
You drive the highways the way you do,
  With trails never ending out there for you.
We grasp a moment, just now and then,
  Yet, I still keep waiting the best I can.

Chorus
Oh! Oh! The nights are lonely.
The days are long.
And I know I love you...
But my dream is gone.
My dream is gone...
Oh! Yes, my dream is gone!
It makes it hard
To carry on...
All because
My dream is gone.
Oh...Yes...My dream is gone.

Now days seem to just come and go,
  Sometimes I hear from you on the road.
My heart tells me this just ain't right;
  That I should just forget you tonight.

My Dream is Gone *(continued)*

Still...From the deepest strand that is left,
  I feel a love that's killing myself.
I will still grasp that moment now and then...
  Still waiting, Babe, the best I can.

Chorus
Oh! Oh! The nights are lonely.
The days are long.
And I know I love you...
But my dream is gone.
My dream is gone...
Oh! Yes, my dream is gone!
It makes it hard
To carry on...
All because
My dream is gone.
Oh...Yes...My dream is gone.

Then the call comes over the phone
  And you tell me you are now far gone.
Now, I know it's really finally over...
  That you no longer will be my lover...
I see your face in the back of my mind...
  I wonder how you can just leave me behind.
Still, your trails you roll take you away
  My love, just remember our first day.

I've Got to Get Over You

The things we said to each other...
　　Brings nothing but trouble...
The heartbreak is coming fast!
　　Perfect love's a moment to not last!
I cannot forget the passionate hours...
　　The quiet little walk in the flowers.
I've lost all control!
　　We have to let go!
This love just won't do...
　　Baby, I have to get over you!

Chorus
　　　　I've got to get over you...
　　　　　　That's what I must do!
　　　　Why do I go insane
　　　　　　At the mention of your name?
　　　　Oh! Yes! I've got to get over you!
　　　　　　Mum-hum! I've got to get over
　　　　　　you!

I've Got to Get Over You *(continued)*

The phone in my pocket rings,
　　When it's you, I drop everything!
Everyone that walks by
　　Sees sadness so deep inside...
I smile through the tears
　　There's an empty deep fear...
For I know how it all goes
　　With a man on the road!
This precious love just won't hold true
　　Baby, I have to get over you!

Chorus
　　　　I've got to get over you...
　　　　　　That's what I must do!
　　　　Why do I go insane
　　　　　　At the mention of your name?
　　　　Oh! Yes! I've got to get over you!
　　　　Mum-hum! I've got to get over
　　　　you!

May Love be with You

The wonders of your tenderness
Are always in my heart
The happiness you've brought to me
Can make the teardrops start.
I can feel you close
When you're not so near
And I know I love you
Even without a fear.

The greatness of your love, my dear,
I never can explain.
I seem to always shiver
Each time I hear your name.
In all our life to come
I never want you blue,
For I love you so dearly
And wish love be with you.

The times that I have let you hold me
Oh, so close to you
The beauty that I see, dear,
In every thing you do.
Times I feel alone
Yet, I know you care.
The brightness of your tender smile
Leaves me unaware.

May Love be with You *(continued)*

Chorus
May Love be with you darling
At each day's end.
May love be with you darling
When the next one does begin.
May love be with you, darling,
When I'm far gone,
May love be with you, darling,
May you go on and on.

Disappointed in Romance

Disappointed in love again
Nobody seems to care
Disappointed in romance
Oh my heart still cares.

When I see you are smilin'
In your picture on the wall
I feel so foolish
Because I had to fall.

Wish I never had met you
Wish you would walk out the door,
Disappointed in love again
I don't need you anymore.

Disappointed in love again
Because you didn't care
Thought you really did love me
What a foolish aire.

Why did you leave me to suffer
Why did you turn me on
My heart is aching
Now, I just can't go on.

My tender heart is aching
To just be held in your arms again
And I need you, my darling,
We were more that just friends.

Chorus
Disappointed in romance
Go on your merry way
Disappointed in love again
I don't want you today.

Do You Ever Think of Me?

Each morning when I rise
  And check out the sky,
My mind turns gently to you
  Wondering what for the moment you do.
I remember places and many times
  Our hearts met with perfect rhyme.
You so gentle, always a wonderful man
  Making me believe I know I can.

Old times past have faded away --
  Like you never entered my day.
Everything now just comes aglow
  For loving you is what I know.
Maybe it's breakfast or delivering the load
  That takes you yonder and down the road.
As my heart leaps heavily as it can be --
  I sit here dreaming, "Do you think of me?"

It's the same old mad rat race
  With days roaring a rugged pace.
I reach for stars wanting you now
  Hope this trip will bring you here somehow.
Reason is unreasonable, you're unforgettable-
  My unfilled passion will never be regrettable.
I remain in the splendor of your need --
  Baby, do you ever think of me?

Chorus

> Yes! Do you ever think of me?
> Am I so blind to believe
> That you drift by now and then
> Reaching to pull me back in?
> Oh, Baby, will it ever be?
> Tell me, do you ever think of me?

Friend

Look! Everything said certainly is true –
The stories they say about you.
You're tough, defiant and strong to end –
A deep giving heart, the best friend.

Carry On

No matter the scale of implication –
No matter the prosperous gravity of indignation –
It seeds the meadow in the Fall –
Saving for Spring the best of all.
And surge with moisture with tears from the eyes
While joyous rainbows arch o'er the tide.
A matter of need to not prolong –
Pick up the pieces and carry on.

Worth Dying For

Never too quick to judge a mate;
    When scrambled time falls on the plate.
Fulfill if you will a minutes awakening
    A project so focused there for taking.

Down the road and by the sea,
    Goes hand in hand touching you and me.
So long to everything outside the door.
    A friend so special, worth dying for.

The Missing Part

What matters if you give your life,
Your body, heart and soul...
That when you reach for a needed hand,
You are left there in the cold.
They play along from time to time
Until the dew of youth is gone,
It breaks your heart to be apart...
Knowing you are not his home.

A blue jay is cruel as he protects
His mate and her young...
Yet the day is near, they disappear
And his duty is now done.
He flies around but never for long
Then by the following spring,
He settles a nest with the best,
To protect his new found dream.

A wasted life for us to live
When love has flown the coop.
To pretend it's there still knowing
It's what's left of the group.
Yet, carry on though love is gone
Away many years ago...
Live in need without the seed
That wills you to follow through.

The Missing Part *(continued)*

It is a start the missing part
That makes you search that dream.
To wander out in the night
Looking for what it must mean.
Heaven oft is so near by
Though as you find that the part missing.
When it's there, and if it's there...
Fumble your way for what it may bring.

Ode to Home

Gloomy bleak gray fossils reach up
  I drip between their unnatural bend.
Seeing faint fog before me trying
  To catch me once again
Even with the bright sun
  That envelopes this clear day
When there is a house I pass
  There are no children at play.

Shrouds of granite cut the view
  That should be velvet mountains blue
Towering over everything else
  That dips deep to it's feet.
Corridors of ridges blast no reason
  It seems nothing really reaps.
There's no harvest of crop surrounding
  The dwellings that are here-in—
You speak to a strange passer-by
  They turn away to great no friend.

The split in the vast divisions
  That loom all around—
Let you know there is nothing
  To pierce this empty sound.
When the stream rolls in the shadows
  That flicker with barren trees –
Makes all of North Carolina beautiful
  And it reveals that mystery!

Say '*Love*'

To some the word comes oh so swift,
  At the first look, if you catch my drift.
They sing it fast, so loud and clear!
It leaves a ringing in the ear!
To some, the word is so hard to form,
  They put it off, afraid of a storm
Not wanting to expose their tender heart,
  They may feel old pain, that plays a part.

To some the word is oh so easy,
  They shout it out, being pleasing.
They find soft words that fondle their needs,
  Intent on capturing special little deeds.
Yet, some wait, holding on to fears,
  Hoping that somehow things will clear.
They find a void when trying to reach out,
  Words won't come, just the same old doubt.

To some the word needs much more meaning,
  They throw it around like a house cleaning.
To everyone they meet it's a constant word...
  After a while, it's only simply heard.
To some, they wish the word 'love' be easy,
  Portray feelings, when lips start freezing.
It makes it crazy with the need to say...
  Then turn it off for another day.

Say *'Love'* (continued)

But whether the word comes easy or not;
  Life plays tricks with this plot.
It really doesn't matter what you do,
  You play your hand for what suits you.
There are no rules or kind of regulation;
  If it gets said none or with multiplication...
The depth of the heart will reveal it, too...
  It is very simple, that, I love you!

Cpl. Glenn Wyatt and K-9, too.
Davidson County Arts Museum

45

PART III

About

Love

Too Much Too Soon

Our love came so fast
We couldn't to stop it,
Our lives and hearts were
So deep entwined.

You said, "I love you"
Before we were ready.
Then the next thing I knew,
You were mine.

Too much too soon,
We were not ready;
Too much too soon,
To really know.

Too much too soon,
We almost married;
Too much too soon,
It had to go.

Dearest Baby

Dearest Baby...
There's no heavier heart than one that's lonely
There is nothing that compares to you only.
You make the sun lift in my sky.
And I chase each butterfly.
My love for you is always sure --
Whatever comes we shall endure.
The thunder of your engines at night --
Keeps you moving along; the pace is right!
I miss the strength from your arms.
I thrive with the gentleness of your charm.
Good overcomes the silence of time,
I'll be here for you, walking the line.
I busy myself each and every day;
Praying real soon you'll drive my way.
The phone rings, I grab it fast!
If it is you...The die is cast!

I'll stop everything and climb to the moon!
Nothing greater than you saying, "See you soon!"
Then, I hold you tight as we do --
I find your lips that are hungry, too!
I feel your heart beating next to mine --
For this moment, it's all perfect, so fine!
Dearest Baby,
Make this end;
Still I hang on again and again.

I'll Never Find Another You

I can't tell you enough about
My heartaches
I can't tell you enough
About my fears.
I won't believe, darling,
That you have left me.
No, never, after
All of these beautiful years.

Don't leave me
Oh, love me, darling.
Tell your heart
What it should do.
Don't leave me
Oh, love me darling.
I'll die before
I find another you.

I can't tell you how much
I feel this empty.
I can't tell you again
About nights I don't sleep.
I won't believe it, darling,
That you have left me.
No longer caring...
I falter swearing each day and weep.

I miss you so much now...
Although I know, darling,
You cannot help that
You had to go.
It's just that I should
Have been able to hold you.
Just a last time
So we both could really know.

I can't tell you enough
About the good times.
I can't forget
Enough about the bad.
So I walk the dirt road
And whistle softly.
I place another rose,
Then turn from your grave, so sad

Ode to Love

It happened on a very cold day,
That he took my hand and led me away,
To a place alone out of town,
Where no one would be, away from sound.
I remember well how he reached to me,
His smile was soft as meant to be.
I thought of nothing but did respond,
Into his arms, my love he won.

Some days later we met once again,
Me and that most wonderful man.
Our love endured time and test,
I think he knew that he was my best.
Our lips touch the minute we meet,
He easily sweeps me off my feet.
I fall apart when I hear his name,
I don't show it, that's the game.

Then years passed by without fail,
Little we heard, occasional mail...
Then, I had a vision that I should see,
If that special man meant so much to me.
A summer trip, then he was there,
In the woods again, touching my hair.
With lips entwined I knew again,
My lover's power, he's my best friend.

Ode to Love *(continued)*

Now, together as it should have been,
It'd been better that it should end.
To the love and dreams we both need,
Without loneliness this special creed.
His sweetness is mine and his tender way,
I respect and love him more each day.
With his love my sun will rise...
I feel it all from his blue eyes.

Let me give all that I have to give,
Let me show you how to live.
In the way we find to have our love,
There will always be plenty more of.
No one can say what time will bring,
Just while we have them let us sing.
The love we share now 'til forever...
Let love flow unleashed as a river!

Hope for Love

With the break of day, I should come alive
to the warmth of your love,
To feel your heartbeat and the heat of your
body entangled with mine.
Reaching to touch your lips with my lips in
sweet soft communion,
And to take you with me to our world of
paradise, an ethereal, pleasure divine.
Do I love you?

Yes, I love you more than words can say,
Each moment you're in my heart grows each day.
Yes, I love you more and more,
With you in my life there's something to live for.
Why pretend?
        I am content.
You are wonderful, so elegant,
So beautiful, so natural and good,
You are even more I know;
I can give you love, if you would
Let the day come that you sap all of my love,
Reach out and touch the heart that is waiting.
Hope for love just here for taking.

Eternal Love

Nothing is quite certain, we should suppose...
   Sometimes love dies like a withering rose,
But it all passes along slowly but sure,
   A new love should be stronger to endure.
What can I give to you?
   I can give you love that would be so tender
A deep warmth that brings your surrender.
   To be your friend throughout our lives
And keep loving you with paradise.
   I know what it is supposed to be...
I have seen death, birth and the in-betweens.
   From this day forth, I promise to be
The dream you find for eternity!

Wealth in Tomorrow

One looks at today with little thought,
and hopes tomorrow will follow through.
He says, I hope and I pray,
It will surround just me and you.
Yet, when the dawn does break,
He cries out to the 'alarm' be still.
But, the moments awakening thoughts appear,
He rises his body against his will.

Just one ten minutes, he wishes at the clock.
It happened, oh, too fast, before total rest.
But he sits to the side of the bed,
In that first coffee, he knows, getting up is best!
For tomorrow here, tomorrow will be gone,
Upon the horizon, another morrow will be.
Now, cover today is the thing on hand,
Once it is the twilight you see.

Oh, for part of yesterday, that slipped
Right through my hands,
Had I half of the yesterdays,
I would be a younger man.
Still, time goes on at its steady pace,
And todays come slipping in.
Then again we have to face
It is gone before it began.

To wish away our little life,
Is a silly thing to do.
For the years grow shorter anyhow,
After you pass twenty-two.
So at the break of dawn each day,
Wouldn't it be an easier thing,
To leap out of bed, brush your teeth,
While hearing that crazy clock ring?

Now that the day arrived,
And I must engage full strength,
I answer the phone and open my mail,
And ponder things at length.
There is much to be had in each moment,
And always nearly too much to do.
I tap my pencil a wicked lick,
And wonder who could wear my shoes!

But, I am happy with this I've chosen
And I am comfortable in every way.
For somehow I know it won't be long
And I will see my sweetheart today.
So as I know the time keeps pushing,
It sometimes strikes me with horror...
I must take the best of every day,
To find the wealth in tomorrow.

Ode to Life

The marks of time are on our face,
Our empty feelings we can't erase.
But think of precious times and place
The victim of it all is haste.

Let sweet love carry you in your mind
To know that it is not all blind,
And be there where you are mine,
Knowing the secrets are so divine.

Life being all the hell it can be,
One speaks loudly of liberty;
Too much a loss to even get free,
It's a dark corner left for you and me.

But shout out love for someone dear
Everyone comes to give a sneer,
Somehow they all think it is queer
That another's love could be so clear.

What kind of habit we seem to live,
Hold out the hand while they give.
Does it take an earthquake to reveal
Without them we'd have to steal?

Ode to Life *(continued)*

Sweeping on goes precious time,
I know that your love is mine...
Without contract or such to bind,
We're together and all is fine.

The hope is nigh, we have our dream,
We know whatever, our hearts are being,
Today full of love is everything,
For tomorrow awaits a golden ring.

The Way I Am

The key to life is 'don't look back',
For there is very little to see...
What is important is ahead...
That is how it was told to me.
But when you have so many hours...
Most of them alone,
It is hard to find the buttercups...
In a simple song.

To fill the day with little things
And block out the bad you see...
It takes quite a person,
And I try to make that person me.
Slip a little happiness where you may,
and seek for simple truth,
And time will fly as it passes by,
Soon, you will leave your youth.

We know that life is a fortune,
the key is to learn to live,
That we might know and we might be,
Someone who loves to give.
To have that time to be alone,
A fortunate person is he...
For in this time you have for thought,
A better person you can be.

One who goes about at a rugged pace,
Has not the time to calculate...
Nor even consider his personal fate...
And loses himself when it's too late.
You have to spend some hours alone...
To be able to follow the tide.
So when you do become thirty,
You are not just in it for the ride.

Chorus
Sometimes it is boring,
Sometimes quite a test,
Sometimes you almost wonder --
Why am I not like the rest?
But in these easy moments,
When you look at yourself and see,
It is much better to be the way I am...
Certainly not like he.

You Make My Day

I hear the alarm,
  It has no charm,
And roll out of bed
  Feeling half dead.
I put coffee on,
  Hear a radio song,
Brush my teeth
  Put socks on my feet;
Bacon starts to fry,
  Time will soon fly...
Kids get into gear,
  At breakfast bend my ear...
An hour is gone,
  I'm home alone,
As I do my face,
  I start another race
Head for town
  And it goes on around!
The clock goes on around!

Then, it's home again
  Touching the lives of those therein...
An empty dream lives deep in my soul,
  A lifeless feeling I can't control.
Just a breath away, you stay,
  Feeling you there, you make my day.

You Make My Day *(continued)*

There is so much to give,
  So much more of life to live.
The despair of yesterday fades,
  With the promise tomorrow gave.
To hold you tightly in the night,
  And cling wildly to our dream and plight.

Yes, I really love you more,
  More yet today than ever before.
We are one heart and one soul,
  One spirit, one body enfolded.
I know now and forever as we play,
  You are what I need to make my day!

          I hear the alarm,
          I feel your charm,
          You are in my bed,
          I caress you instead,
          You turn me on
          as the radio plays our song...
          I hold you tight
          and pray for the plight
          to be the woman you need,
          without self and foolish greed.
          I bury my soul with you
          with a promise to be true.
          As we depart our separate way
          we're still there, you make my day!

Burning Tongue

You hear of burning...
What score be cast?
Should it not take a form of learning?
Would that be best?
You all have heard, the long old tale...
Of burning bridges behind, and do it well.
Why not cast the anchor deep in the sea?
That's another way to run from me!

A few words can heat a simple grave...
Yet, how piercing the sound they made.
That burning sensation in the heart...
So easy to make, the trembles start.
Did you ever check to see how wrong
Before it's told and you carry on?
Shelter from the twisted tears
Will never retract down the years...
That rudely shred the easy calm...
They never be less than a bomb!

The injured who obstruct the very force...
Only feel that burning, of course.
Think again, maybe real deep;
Burning words will loose your sleep.

Burning Tongue *(continued)*

A tongue should proudly be put to leash...
Than let loose words for you to reap.
Dare the daring, when you rest,
Find the quiet from the contest.

You can always find ransom in time to be...
Handle that burning very carefully.
Simple to lash cutting bondage...
In twisted moments of rage.
Hold back! Hang on! Let it wait...
Just do it, for your own sake!
A burning tongue can be taught to employ,
A less tradition than to destroy.
Give thought, and try to see...
Just the trouble a tongue can be!

Attitude so smart suggests hateful glares;
Sets you back with whispers and stares.
Burning tongues never look ahead...
Just makes its' presence for others to dread.
You don't get by with forked-mouth...
You don't even win! You just loose out!
All that comes, that seemed so smart,
Your burning tongue, burned out the heart.

Ode to Growing Up

Time slips past with endeavors each day,
We while the time with importance, as we play.
At moments, we flashback to old forgotten dreams,
Reaching out frantically to see what it could mean.
But in the scale for reaching heights you know.
Everyday you climb closer for love or show.
Why complain at all, if your life is a myth?
Were the stars you clung to, just a barren kiss?

As a child, we shivered when sent away to school;
There, they said, "It's learning, the golden rule."
We carry on and tackle this fate,
Our hearts beating wildly to meet the pace.
With books open and at times under your arm,
You looked behind, seeing frivolous charm.
A cautious smile and maybe, a sneak of a wink,
Your face flushes a signal, as it turns sort of pink.

Now, it's time to forge ahead, still being brave,
It turns into autumn, that first day to rave,
"We are about to arrive in the junior high,
It is much more important than just being alive!"
Once there, a heavier rule; pushing, yet learning;
Trying, growing, changing and earning.
Just a smile, more cautious than before,
Blow a kiss in the wind, as I pass your door.

Ode to Growing Up *(continued)*

Years slipped by...
Now we're seniors vowing friendship forever!
Scamper thru a last year, just before heaven.
I would hear your name, see you in the halls,
Deep in my heart, I dreamed you might call.
But all that slipped past us; secret yearnings.
Focused on careers, unknown fires burning.
To forget old passions, what never would be,
And pass into the world seeking to be free!

The world of time built walls between us all...
At we failed, but got up from our falls.
We turned into teachers, doctors and nurses...
Writers, lawyers, preachers, whatever the curses.
We found mates; extended home-fronts, too.
Over the years, I'd think memories of you.
At times I'd wonder where your life had turned,
Were you handsome, strong, unconcerned?

(continued to next page)

The letter came saying, "We're all to meet...
Bring your spouse or loved one; find a seat."
I toiled with the picture of seeing you again...
At last, I pulled it together to see you walk in!
I felt that same feeling of a million days ago...
'I never got to say yes, I never got to say no.
Now we're both alone, under a big moon...
We smiled and talked a natural tune
Taking hands, our lips finally kiss
And share a sweet moment of virtuous bliss.

Flashback!
      Flashback!
            Flashback!
                  Now! Now! Now!

Shelter Me

The fire of day broke through with light
I imagined you there touching the sight
Wonderful memories shed such great peace
The billions of blessings reveal its grace.
And as I roam this whole world over
You make it happen even when I'm roving.
Our alliance so fair, so grand indeed
Always knowing you care in time of need.

(continued to next page)

Shelter Me *(continued)*

We get weary it seems everyday just trying
The ups and downs are not hiding.
There are saints walking here among us
Still two-faces prodding against our trust;
The wicked ease on intent to spy,
That our best we do is always on trial.
I've known forever the face of the devil
And turn in haste that God will level.

Chorus
    Shelter me with love
    Shelter me in your passion
    Shelter me from fear
    Give me shelter lasting.
    Oh, God hold me safe
    As I tremble along the way
    Oh, God lead through
    As I search for my place.
    That place we call home
    Above this old world
    The place in your kingdom
    Where you reign ever more!

IF YOU ARE SEARCHING FOR
THE VERY __BEST__ IN FURNITURE TRANSPORTATION
YOU ONLY NEED TO MAKE ONE CALL.
1-800-777-2583
SHELBA D. JOHNSON TRUCKING, INC.
CAN GIVE YOU THE SERVICE THAT YOU NEED TO EVERY
CITY IN EVERY STATE ON THE EASTERN SEABOARD OR TO
LOUISANA OR TEXAS OR TO INDIANA, ILLINOIS, MICHIGAN
OR OHIO. WE HAVE YOU COVERED WITH EXCELLENT
EQUIPMENT, SERVICE, AND RATES

SJD
JOHNSON
TRUCKING

Shelba D. Johnson
Trucking, Inc.
Thomasville, N.C.

1640 BLAIR ST.
THOMASVILLE, N.C. 27360
PHONE 336-476-2000
WATS 800-777-2583

IF YOU HAVE SAFE DRIVING SKILLS AND AN EXCELLENT
ATTITUDE AND WOULD LIKE TO WORK FOR THE VERY
__BEST__ CONTACT OUR COMPANY AT
1-800-777-2583 TO SET UP AN INTERVIEW.

PART IV

Things

of

Life

I'd Like to Be...

I'd like to be a queen,
　　　Sitting by your throne,
Serving you with grandeur
　　　As you carry on.
I'd like to be a kitty cat
　　　Laying by your door
Waiting for you to come and play
　　　And pet you some more.
I'd like to be a diamond
　　　Twinkling on your hand
Watching as you do your task
　　　And proving you really can.
I'd like to be a butterfly
　　　On the wind of your every day
That when you see me you're happy
　　　And make a difference they say.

Little Girl, You're Changing
(To my daughter, Rebekah, at age 14)

Little girl, you're changing,
From a child to womanhood.
Your smile is sweeter,
And you're looking so good!
For years you were mine,
And I was there for you;
But little girl, you're changing...
Like all little girls do!

Today I see you smiling
As you stand before me...
Your eyes are flashing,
Those womanly dreams.
And you look into a mirror...
And I know that you see,
Little girl, you are changing...
You are no longer my baby.

Now I look down the road
And see castles in the sky;
As I touch your hair, darling,
I see how time did fly...
And it's all like a dream
That day you were born,
Little girl, you are changing,
As you weather the storm!

Now, here you are standing
In your elegant best,
Competing in this cold world,
Reaching out to meet the test.
You're beautiful and laughter,
You're everything to me!
Little girl, you are changing...
Something wonderful to see!

Little girl, my big girl...
My childly gorgeous woman!
This moment we share,
This moment we remember...
Yesterday, today, tomorrow,
Forever to reign!
Little girl...You changed
Into this elegant beauty queen!

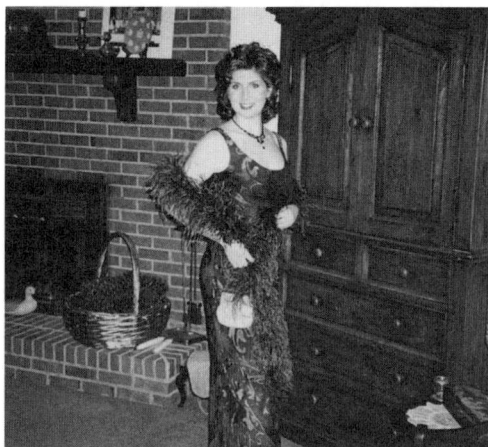

Let's go Fishing!

I looked out the window;
Clear sky I could see.
Would be such a perfect day
For just you and me!
I thought of the ocean,
I thought of the sand,
I thought of a trout stream
And you as a fisherman.

I could see to myself
A tangled mass of line,
'Cause I remembered,
Putting up the pole of mine.
Still, it only takes a moment
To get everything all set,
I kiss my love and make a wish
To the stream and make my bet!

I love to feel a cool breeze
Stirring across my cheeks,
Listen to birds flutter past,
See their chirping beaks!
Yet, of all the wonder in it,
As along our path we're moving,
The freeness and beauty in the land
The biggest part of fishing.

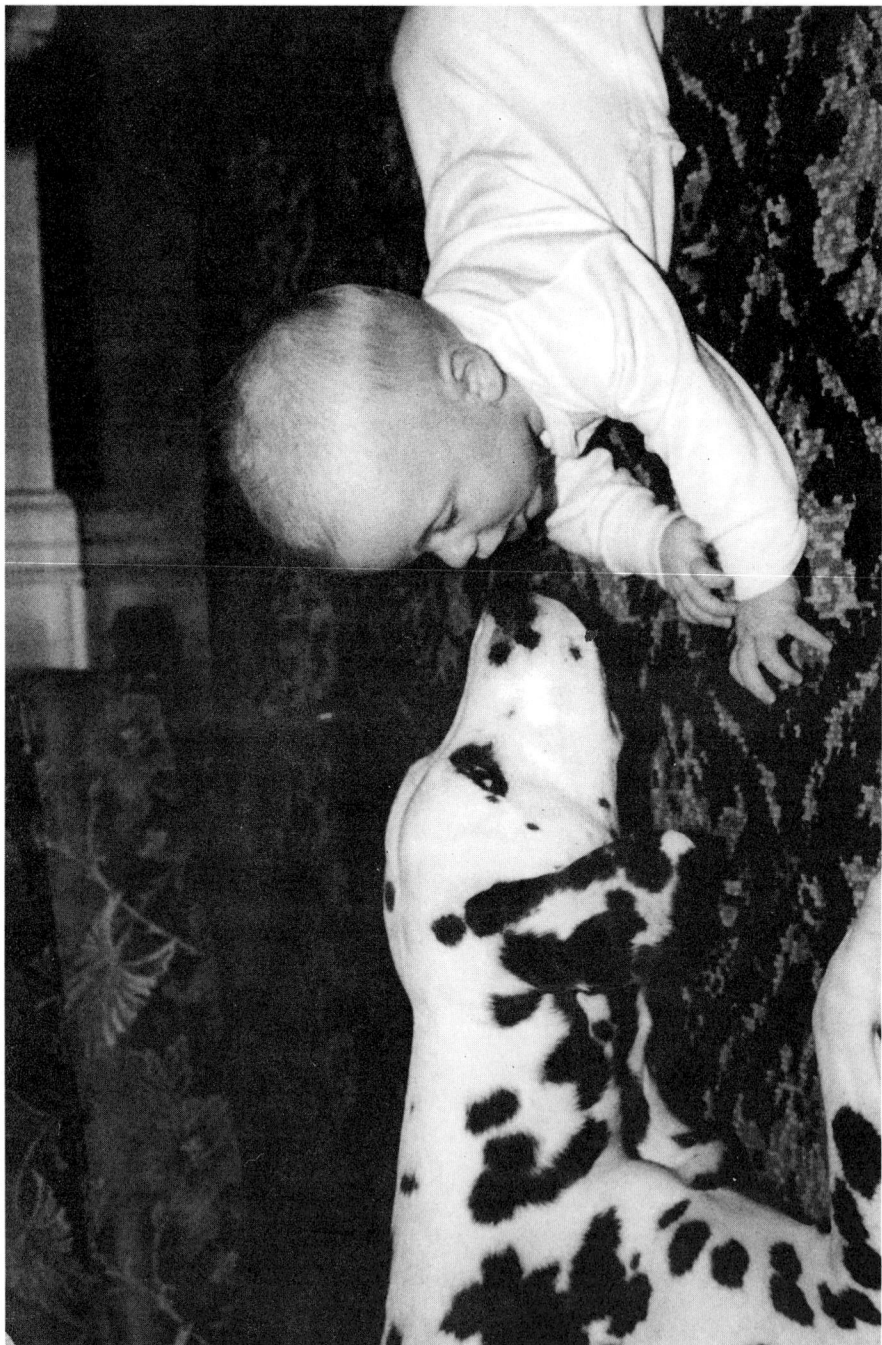

Isaac Hunt and Casey

Me and Casey
(Dedicated to my grandson, Isaac)

Once upon a time
    Miss Casey was mine!
Oh, that precious Dalmatian
    Could rule every emotion!
Someday I'll take a marker pen
    As any boy might try thinking.
I'll connect those 'spots'
    Making her stripped, why not?
Yet, I stare into her face --
    Guess I like those 'dots' in place.
She takes her nose and pushes me around
    Like I'm a puppy she found.
I look at her, she looks at me,
    We're best friends, me and Casey.

The Happy Horse

One day I walked through the park...
Things were closed, it was getting dark.
The birds still chirping in the trees,
Made me feel happy as I could be.
I saw through a fence in the park zoo...
A strange animal; he looked at me, too.
He looked rather different I thought, indeed;
Sort of like a horse with a hump he didn't need.
His ears were long and eyes very brown...
His expression was serious, sort of a frown.
I said, "Oh, animal, gracious sakes alive!
You're so very lucky. I had to work 'til five!"
He smiled back and gave a great big snort
Saying, "It's great I'm not people.
You're all a real worry wart!"

Naughty Doggie

I saw a naughty doggie
Sitting in the park.
Then I saw the lady
Standing in the dark.
It was very obvious
What Doggie had to do...
The sign there saying --
"Keep Animals off; It Means YOU!"
Naughty lady! Shame!
You should read the sign!
If I fall at play into 'IT'.
That would be a crime.

The Owl Egg

If an owl left an egg for me
   In the hollow of a pine tree
I would ever, ever grateful be
   Nor tarnish her nest even gently.
Yet, still the thought of baby blue eyes
   So round and perfect seeming wise
I think I'll leave her speckled eggs be,
   And stay from her nest in the tree.

Into the Night

I lost my way into the night,
No streets were in sight.
I heard funny noises calling,
It seemed I was all right.
Then I remembered once more,
I wasn't there alone.
Someone walked there with me,
Together, we travel on.
I lost my way into the night,
What really must I do?
Maybe sit, think and meditate,
Daylight will see us through.

Natural and Free

When I look in your eyes
And you're holding me.
Life is wonderful
I feel natural and free!

Natural and free,
Yes, natural and free.
That's how it must be --
Loving natural and free.

When you touch my lips
Whispering you love me,
It's all so swell
We're natural and free!

Natural and free,
Yes, natural and free.
That's how it must be --
Loving natural and free.

Changes

Pass the salt; pass the time
   Pass the word; pass with mind.
Shake the salt; shake the time
   Shake the word; shake the mind.
Melt the salt; melt the time
   Melt the word; melt the mind.

Road Rage

Oops! There they go!
    Carrying on like they know
Immoral loops intent on race –
    Not caring who they deface.
No memory of time or of the past
    Just cut 'em off, go alas!
Toot the horn, shake the fist!
    Stick out the tongue – it's a risk!
Swerve the vehicle, right then left –
    Crawl on a bumper to spite their-self.
Push and shove, a possible free will –
    Maybe its all an indignant thrill.
Even so, come what may –
    They keep on, day after day.
Someone turns off just to give in –
    Leaving the other with a 's'-eatin' grin.
The tragedy of a stupid mind –
    It goes nowhere but in a bind.
No purpose served
    No kind of success –
Just some big fool
    Creating a mess!
Thoughts of roaring into a rage –
    Might just put you in a cage!

By the Sea

I walk by the sea to find the calm,
But it's angry waves lash out at my feet.
I look beyond the anger to find deep serenity;
And a silent secret retreat.
A boat sets sail to the soft flowing wind
And the birds of the evening return home.
A journey no where from somewhere in my past
Nurses peace to my soul to belong.

And as I walk by the sea I seek
To look even farther than before!
That any restless minute spent
Sings golden thoughts forevermore.
Upon the evening shadows that cross
The walk of our lives,
I will kneel and whisper a prayer
That quickly and quietly take us by.
And unto the time we have had
And the future that is yet to be...
I reach out for your gentle hand
And pray hard you will be there for me.

I walk by the sea, alone and free;
Wishing so hard for you and me...
That the shallow waters of harsh
Spoken words will mellow within,
And that your strength and love

By the Sea *(continued)*

Will be mine once again.
No words spoken or fancy deeds done
Can replace the magic of you,
Nor can it ever go on forgotten.
The depth of my love...It's true!

So I walk by the sea, trying to forget,
Only to remember vivid love...
And as I depart for home, alone
With trouble heart, I seek strength from above.
There is no world with fancy parties
Or the charm that I knew yesterday;
It is bleak and dim involved with forgetting,
And in the wee hours for us, I still pray.

Suzi Lee

You packed your things and went away
Told me you'd be back someday...
I felt for sure.
Then friends of mine told me...
They saw you eating at the place we used to be.
So I went down there the very next night...
My eyes could hardly believe the sight...
You and Suzi Lee...
Her, wrapped up in your voice
and arms so hungrily...
I felt heat rush to my head
I wished that I were dead...
I wept for sure...
I looked again to believe my eyes...
Then turned away.
I walked into our home with the familiar key...
I told my sister go on home...
I'm all right this way.
I held our son the age of two...
Too young to know we had lost you
And wept the pain away...
Tomorrow is here and gone...
We are still all alone...
You didn't return...
Told me, friends of mine,
You were drunk and committed a crime...
The courts forgave...But...Go away...
Too much is past...The boy is are mine,
We are getting along just fine...
Suzi Lee got married, too...You are alone...
And I'm still Mama and Papa in our happy home.

Again

Each moment may be an eternity
That fills our worthwhile need.
To breath erotic pleasure incredible
And link with its pleasurable seed.
To speak softly sweet words
With keen overtures and meaning
To just give love for the taking
Shallow of the natural greed.

A good song may be an answer
To heal the heartbeat's insight.
To know erotic pleasure is incredible
And feel its' peaceful height!
To love softly with sweet words,
With overtones of being right;
To bow down to the surface
And cry out into the night!

I feel my arms as they tremble;
When I know I must have you go --
To have had incredible erotic pleasure
And know I love you so.
To speak sweet words softly
Stay brave and let you flee --
With everything that has happened,
You must come, then go free.

Then, I felt life slipping away again.
Just please one more day again!
Then stop it all and pray again
Now, begin all over again!

Ode to Justice
(From <u>Red High Heels II</u>)

When your faith is shattered, life stands still,
Nothing much matters, seems all is over the hill.
Fringes of dreams that really could come true, .
It might take time; near dying before the real issue
When all else fails and your patience goes thin,
Outside the realm encircled kicks the real tiger in.

They take your heart, eat away at your soul,
Spell their emotions, try to steal your control.
Money seemed important before that time
Go out for banquets while you socially climb.
The rug's snapped beneath, clinging not to fall,
You look around, but there's almost no one at all.

They blow fear, savage vice, you tremble inside,
'Til one day it happens, you cut loose to go hide.
Time takes its toll, rules your head to your hands;
Someday they deserve one final dance.
Finally, once and for all! The hell is ended at last.
Big tiger call on those who laid trail from the past

A big tribute to justice finally well done.
Hallelujah, it's over, the tiger has won!
They line up the devils, march them to their tune,
Put them away now, like they tried doing to you.
Sing out freedom with deliverance, lift the vale!
The tiger stalks his prey, marching them to hell!
But patience and time, may liberty bring,
Because there is a tiger caring for you and me.
Hallelujah, it's over, the tiger has won!

The Writer

I may not be famous
    Or public in any way.
It really doesn't matter
    I just go on to say,
Things everywhere squires a meaning
    I jot it down like it's seeming.

End

The gaiety of life
    Stalks for fun
To find those playing
    Bright in the sun.
Tidbits of laughter
    Overwhelms the soul
While moments of sorrow
    Reach to control.
A silhouette of time
    Strikes the magic hour
Ruling everything crazy
    Searching for power.
But as all else comes
    Eventually it goes
The flower comes to bud
    And finally a rose.
A shower sprinkles cool
    To drop as a friend
There are certain conclusions
    With each things' end.

ABOUT THE AUTHOR

Rotha Dawkins was born in Lexington, NC. She is a graduate of Lexington High School. While still a student, and just eighteen years old, she held the first fashion show in Lexington with twenty-five gowns which she had made and designed. The show was sponsored by Belk-Martin store and promoted statewide. Rotha received scholarships and awards for this endeavor. She then went to New York University and Mayer School of Dress Design in New York City. There she received a degree in draping and design.

Rotha has had custom design studios in New York, Great Falls, MT; Riverside, CA; Seattle, WA; Winston Salem, Greensboro, Lexington, Thomasville and Asheboro, NC.

In Seattle, she owned and operated *Rotha's Commercial Design* where she manufactured and designed hotel, motel and business uniforms. Also, while in Seattle, she had her own television series, "Sewing for Profit" and it was derived from her talk show, "Fashion News on TelePrompTer."

Her book, Sewing for Profit, was a sell out and is in the process of being published again.

Rotha has two children:

Son, William Hunt, a fireman for Lexington Fire Department, and his wife, Faith, is a nurse at Lexington Memorial Hospital. Their son, Isaac Palmer, is Rotha's true incentive and their daughter, Grace Roland, is Rotha's live doll.

Daughter, Rebekah Ruth Tredway is married to son-in-law Chad Gallimore, who is with U.P.S. and is one of the main 'recipe-testers.' Rebekah, an executive personal recruiter for Moses Cone Hospital in Greensboro, NC, is a graduate of High Point University.

At a point, Rotha owned and operated *Rotha's Formal and Tuxedo* in High Point, Thomasville and Asheboro, NC.

She has been director for North Carolina Model Pageants since 1984. Each pageant instructs approximately 45 girls in the areas of modeling and self presentation. Ms. Dawkins directs and attends to individual photo shoots and is mistress of ceremonies for the final program events.

Rotha also designed a line of lingerie, "Le' Joy" and was designer for Neshia in New York, Greensboro Mfg. and Jenny Prince Originals. In New York she modeled for the John Azar Agency in Manhattan.

Ms. Dawkins owned and operated Your Treasure Furniture, shipping furniture to New York and eastern North Carolina.

Rotha is an author, writing novels for the trucking industry, a book of poetry, cookbooks and creates short items for various media.

Over the years, she has been written up in most major state newspapers and magazines. She has been on most radio and television stations as a guest, along with current event projects. She was on Johnny Carson's "Who do you Trust" and several other New York shows. Currently, she hits the path lecturing and autographing.

Rotha owns *La Parisienne* bakery and vintage-fine styled clothing at 211 South Main Street in Lexington, NC. The name of the shop means "The French Thing" -- easy come, easy go theme. Her writing studio is in this same location.